LIFE
&
OTHER
ILLUSIONS

LIFE
&
OTHER
ILLUSIONS

SOURAV G ROY

Anecdote
Publishing House
For the love of quality reading!

Anecdote Publishing House
2nd Floor 2/15 Lane no. 2 Ansari Road, Daryaganj-110002
Email: info@anecdotepublishinghouse.com
Website: anecdotepublishinghouse.com

Published by Anecdote Publishing House
Copyright © Sourav G Roy

First Edition 2025
ISBN 978-81-973806-8-6
MRP ₹ 299

All Rights Reserved.
No part of this publication may be reproduced, stored in a retrieval system, or transmitted in any form, or by any means—electronic, mechanical, photocopying, recording or otherwise—without the prior permission of the publisher. Opinions expressed in it are the author's own. The publisher is in no way responsible for these.

Book Promoted and Marketed by Champ Readers Pvt. Ltd.
Cover design by The Book Bakers
Layout by Graphic Tailor
Printed by Thomson Press (India) Ltd, New Delhi

To my loving son, Dev, whose innocent
spirit fills my heart with
endless joy.
In loving memory of my dear parents.
To my cherished nephew and nieces, may you
find inspiration and hope within these lines.
To my family, I offer my deepest gratitude ,for
their support and encouragement.
To my dearest friends, who have always
been by my side.

Contents

Dawn	1
Dust	3
Homeward	5
The Distant Call	7
Shackled Religion	9
Vacuum	11
Forgotten Shadows	13
The Hypocrite	15
The Wait	17
Slave	19
The Final Journey	21
Lament Of A Father	23
Hathras-Death Of Humanity	25
My Songs Of Freedom	27
A Poem For You	29

Insecure Conscience	31
Aimless	33
Contradictions	35
Nights Of Forgiven Curses	37
Hope	39
The River Inside	41
Speck Of Cloud	43
Beautiful Pain	45
Journey	47
Ode To You….Imperfect Rock	49
Eternal Wars	51
Fantasies In Utopia	53
Broken Masks	55
Surrender	57
The Vanquished	59
Idle Offerings	61
Confessions Of The Faithless	63
Confessions 1	65
Neglected Hopes	67
The Wait	69
Farewell Song	71

Untitled	73
The Broken	75
Days & Nights	77
Faceless Union	79
Unburdened	81
Meandering	83
The Lost Road	85
Stan!	87
Finding Hope	89
In Search Of Reasons	91
Conversation With Walls	93
Lashings Of Guilt	95
Kabul	97
Lost Conscience	99
Lost Reminiscence	101
The Poet	103
Price Of Existence	105
Contradictions	107
The Lies Within Us	109
Ruins	111
Acknowledgements	113

Dawn

As the restless dawn pierced my broken dream

On the lifeless bed I lay, my mind in burdened illusion.

Your vision, alive , then fading into oblivion

A momentary flight from solitude.

Emotion's gentle touch, the fearless wandering of laughter…

My desperate attempt, my last wail to hold on

to a fleeting moment.

Floating in the sea of ecstasy

I gazed upon heaven above

As my weary eyes welcomed the dew of helpless sighs

With the mild taste of tears, passion's last drop on my withered lips.

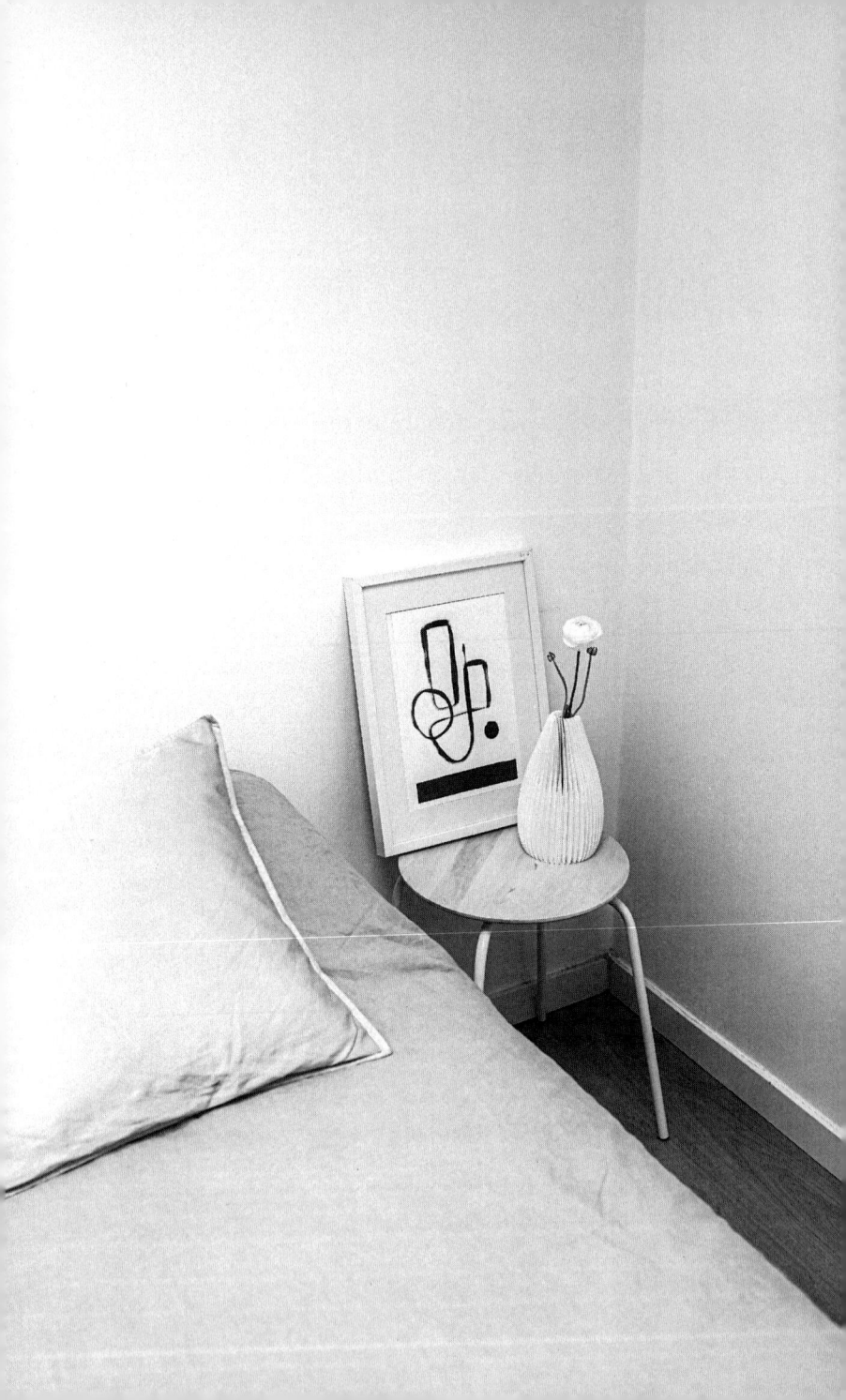

Dust

A speck of dust on the lost corner of the bed,
Faint glimpse of your faded name.
A sweet taste of laughter,
Vanishes with a desperate cry in the blink of an eye.
The teardrop of a lost dream,
Like vapour, lost, in the sky, forever
Still left are the fragments of the day,
Left is the feeling of emptiness, a gentle curse of despair.

Homeward

On these endless roads I walk, through the curse of ruins

My feet embrace the thorns as storms tear me down.

No tears for my eyes, no hunger for my soul

On these nights of hopeless dreams, fearless I lie.

Faith's burden on my shoulders, my wounds lie in peace

Taunted by faint memories, my parched lips wear a smile.

I've heard boastings of tyrants, seen colours of deceit

My mornings lay heavy with the visions of the dead.

In a moment I will fall in the arms of destiny

In your smile I will cherish eternity.

My lifeless legs dragged by unseen chariots

Triumph paints the vision of a broken home.
Remember me child, in your feeble desperations
My journey begins as freedom beckons.

---

*Indian migrant workers ,during the COVID-19 pandemic faced multiple hardships. With factories and workplaces shut down due to the lockdown imposed in the country, millions of migrant workers had to deal with the loss of income, food shortages and uncertainty about their future. Following this, many of them and their families went hungry. Thousands of them then began walking back home, with no means of transport due to the lockdown- Wikipedia

The distant Call

I fly towards the call of the distant meteor
Insignificant chores forgotten by mythical dreams.
No hesitant wisdom can bind me
In freedom , my destiny floats rudderless.
My mind plays the shadow of my soul
My inhibitions lost in fearless devotion.
Restless sins drowned in forgiving seas
I sing songs of wondrous ecstasy.
Your echoed curses lie vanquished
Your `barbed slurs forgiven.
No more tears for the weary hopes
Limitless Peace rests in curious wait.

Shackled Religion

In these shackles of my caged existence

My breath lies heavy, my dreams distant, in chains.

My spirit soars in the innocent blue skies

As weary fingers long for the virgin canvas.

The mind waits in silence, to hear the sounds of fearless laughter

As the heart yearns to break these invisible masks of deceit.

My mind, in search of unbroken innocence

While I fall, ravaged by these barbed rules and bonds.

Your gentle commandments now proclaimed in shrieks

As tyrant logic swallows the remnants of sanity.

My strength takes flight, my voice grows faint,

Yet do I hear the clamour of hope flow from a lost land?

Vacuum

Like an aimless cloud I float, my burden of existence, shunned!

Through the touch of desolate emotions, I see the wheels of time lay in ruins.

Infinite formless truth rebel through the rainbow of reflections,

Reality shines, yet silently I row on the streams of illusion.

Memories hide in fields of imagination, as tears fade,

Yet why does the mind wake up afresh, to the distant call of a child's laughter?

The curious soul pulls open the shattered door of the heart,

The final temptation, for a touch of flawed bliss.

Forgotten shadows

Maybe someday, when my shrivelled fingers open those lost pages

Your name will smile upon the fleeting shadows.

The glitter in my eyes will welcome a weary smile

As silent sighs will float upon memories adrift.

I'll journey for a moment to touch paradise And forget the endless curse of despair.

I'll stare at the faded letters hidden in the worn out box

And search for forgotten words of desire.

Stay, for a while in my world of fantasy

And hold me in your forgiving arms.

Before I fall to ruthless reality,

Set me free…..

The Hypocrite

Here's my confession – I've lived a life of lies,
My lofty morals and lessons in faith,
My love for the feeble, for whom my heart ached.
The fake smiles that vanished every time you left my side,
Layered masks ruled rampant over my shrivelled soul,
Your beliefs crushed by my invisible hands.
Hopes that were fuelled by my careful deceit,
Tender dreams floated by my ruthless schemes,
I've sold hatred with my army of the blind faithful.
Covered my failures with deafening songs of valour,
Blamed you when you raised your feeble voice,
Played with my decorated excuses to break your resolve.

Here I stand accused, my eyes too weak for you,
The smoke of my burning sins choke me at last,
This is my confession, your beliefs, my pretension!
For I have failed to follow my own sermons,
　Judgement passed – "Hypocrite!"

The wait

I tread softly, to cross these ragged boundaries,
My strange imaginations betray buried passion,
Failed by the touch of cheap courage,
I lie helpless , bound by these invisible bonds.
Your sermons lie flat, your dreams unwanted,
In solitude, I've embraced the punisher's hands,
Warm remorse plays devil with broken aspirations,
Bloodied by belief, I've found peace in these shackles.
My mind, in eternal silence as untamed waves lashed,
Painted the night with your vague reflections,
As season's change, my search for you take flight,
Your lost name, discovered in the nightingale's song.
When ruthless Time torments my soul,

Will I find solace in your warm breath,
And so I wait on these lost shores,
For life's blind judgement, for salvation!

Slave

The hour is near, the calls of Freedom grow loud,
My wings take shape through my effervescent eyes.
These merciless shackles feel my last embrace,
Your unforgiving touch, a bond finally ruptured.
My intrepid eyes will greet the new morning Sun,
Free from your eyes that spewed venom.
The gust of rain will wash away my river of tears,
These wounds will breathe absent trauma.
Those shattered dreams will fill my restless heart,
Those buds of withered emotions will bloom.
Maybe lost love will hold out it's forgiving arms,
And caress me, the hurt a distant echo…
My unbridled joy fails to hide behind the broken face
Fleeting moments whisper, yet tonight….I'm a slave!

The final journey

My mind bathed in the violent seas
My valiant ship broken by ruthless waves
I've counted the stars in the spotless nights
As the whales called out in symphony.
In the lap of the highest peaks I've laid
Desperations lost in the arms of purity
Lost in blizzards, I've sung songs of life
In the shadows of forgiveness, I've dismissed envy.
In the thickest of forests, the taste of nectar I've found
In the tired dusk I've run with listless fireflies
Heard the laments of the ancient tree
Amidst perfection, I've gathered specks of curses.
My thirst quenched by the scorching desert sands
Intoxicated by illusions, I've surrendered
As the Sun scorched my broken skin

I've crossed Hell, ravaged the calls of destiny.

And now it's time to say goodbye
Away from fake civilization
The path, unknown, calls my name
The rainbow in its splendour, beckons…

Lament of a Father

When your songs of innocence fog my memories
The tears flow in endless loop.
My strength betrayed, as I fall apart
I hold you in desperation, lost in space.
When the storm rages with all its might
My tired soul haunts my restless sleep.
I wonder if your mercy will free my curse
And you'll remain hidden in my imperfect world.
Often, I lose myself in the stories that we shared
Your toys lie silent in the box of rust.
Do you hear my sermons and tales of life
From my lost home, where I roam, forgotten.
When you find the book of lost words
Remember me, for the times I held you in my arms.

Hathras-Death of Humanity

My blood stains bear no name

Born to be forgotten in your mighty world.

For all I wanted was to spread my wings and fly

To touch those dreams that I delicately nourished.

The claim of humanity touched my frail lips
Freedom's illusion ,for a moment felt true.

My simple mind played by your web of lies

Your generosity reeked of deceit.

When your spotless arms ravaged my soul

Did you hide behind your fragile pride?

In death I saw your savage hatred

In death , my existence lay insignificant.

Now the noise will flow again
While the toothless voices roar.
And soon restless memories will fade
Crushed by the ruthless wheels of time.
Justice will wake from its slumber
Into the arms of shattered hopes.

On 14 September 2020, a 19-year-old Dalit woman was gang-raped in Hathras district, Uttar Pradesh, India, by four upper caste men. She died two weeks later in a Delhi hospital. Her body was cremated by the policemen and her relatives were not allowed to perform the last rites as per the Hindu tradition.

My songs of freedom

I plan to sing my songs of freedom, unrealised
Break the trance, before my dreams fade into the mist.
Unlearn those lessons of worthless patterns
I know my imperfections, I'm running from your trials.
Your spears graze my skin, your gaze burns my soul
Still the songs of revolution flow out of swollen emptiness.
Into the horizon of open dreams where perfections do not rule
And fearless desires roam the streets of our mind.
So I travel to that life of painless solitude
From the listless crowds of loneliness.
Into the realms of endless bliss I flow
Hate's venom long forgotten.
Through these helpless emotions
Straying away into your forgotten world.

A Poem for You

When the morning comes, my words will flow for you

The pages of my mind will search for the stories adrift

Your presence, hidden behind the curtain of dreams

In my exploration, to the lost inspirations will I surrender.

If my words grow thin when the poems call

And illusions mix colours of memories and reality

When my conscience pulls me back home

Remind me, in your drifting thoughts that we're strangers.

When the letters betray my unwritten songs

And tears play softly with the faded words

Covered in the blessings of desperation

I'll seek solace in your fleeting smile.

If my chaotic thoughts paint these poems
And titles search for your name
Perhaps in surrender I'll discover joy
I'll let the paper boat carry my eternal hopes.

Insecure Conscience

Your words of ridicule, your insults unmask you
 For this I know, that deep inside, you're insecure.
Your false pride and your veiled ambitions
They blind you, you're too frail to see the truth.
To the corner I am pushed by your hapless reason
Yet you fail to see my non-existent walls.
Your cuts may bleed me, but I'm still standing
Your weapon of lies too blunt, for me to fall.
For I am free, no burden I carry in my conscience
I may fall but I will rise in stubborn persistence.
My spirit obstinate, my soul unbroken
Bring me the war, for my faith is my shield!

Aimless

In search of my unfinished ambitions
I travel far and wide in the maps of my mind.
I lose sight every now and then, I stumble
Reach out for a hand to hold me up.
I lose faith, lose hope, blind incandescence
In your faded smile I find the colours of belief.
So I run from the hopeless loves
Only to feel nature's endless solitude.
Afraid to show the emotions that hide
Deep inside the fractured house.
I'm running, I'm floating, unrestrained
Forever cursed, forever blessed, forever broken.

Contradictions

…..and then there's Hope,
that strikes me in unexpected ways
scrapes the layers of reality
from my trampled skin.
…..and where's hope
when hopeless prayers fail
teases before it flies away
from my midnight dreams.
…..and there's the morning sun
that still bathes me in bliss
and leaves me just before
he frail goodbyes.
…..and then there's you
present in every breath
and distant with every sigh
haunting illusion of your smile.

Nights of Forgiven Curses

On this night of endless hope and listless fears

I come to you, do you see my faith shining strong

Or do you still fill your mind with unbroken doubts

Cover your eyes, afraid to forgive lost transgressions.

In these times of undying desires and savage hunger

I come to you, for salvaging the broken bonds

Does your hate still rule your conceited kingdom

And tender thoughts lie hidden in your invincible prison.

On these empty roads where once we searched for the dreams

Can we search for the lost thoughts and dried up tears

Can we still hide under the ancient tree when the rain comes

And feel those forgotten sounds of tender whispers.

In this hour of silent sighs and weary prayers

When the calls of surrender torture our souls

Will you take hold of my shrivelled hands

And lay me down, free me from the curse.

Hope

The sky in all its glory, drenched in the blue
My mind , stunned in absolute truth.
On these new wings my dreams soar
The world of envy and fear forever lost.
Nature blessed in perfect harmony
No goal too distant on these vibrant roads.
Loneliness lost in the pages of history
No helpless thoughts in freedom's empty cradle.
In the arms of time will this these footprints disappear
My existence, caressed by the call of the horizon.

The river inside

I have tried and failed to decipher

The fascinating dimness of my mind's projections.

Illuminated by my ignorant ambitions,

Shattered by multitudes of reckless thoughts & desperations!

A vague representation of bright nihilism,

Dotted with silver linings.

Perhaps a step towards salvation, or hope,

Yet clinging to the absurdities of life

An inexplicable balancing act!

Speck of Cloud

You float alone on the spotless blue canvas
No burden on your shoulders, lost in fragment.
Not afraid of the unknown heavens
Forever free from the invisible bonds.
Aimless, you drift, bereft of the shackles of time
No reckless ambitions to weigh you down.
In ecstasy we close our eyes to the misty sun
I float with you, in my dreams of lost expectations.
Somewhere in this perfection, our thoughts embrace
My heart searches for a piece of your empty soul.
Someday, when our paths meet
You'll cleanse me with your drops of rain.
Or maybe, on a summer's day
Forgotten, we'll find shelter in the arms of the Universe.

Beautiful Pain

Beautiful Pain, where have you been?
I've been searching for those moments
When your touch healed my scars.
I see you now, sitting beside me,
Your touch still distant, why do you smile?
Or do you wait for me to explore your endless boundaries?
Beautiful Pain, you're closer than the closest friends,
You define existence, my demons calmed by your breath,
We're like lovers, you're a river that flows in my veins.
I've been wrong, my struggle to hide from your gaze,
Blindly scorned, like a sin, hidden in the darkest corners,
But now I see you, your faithful glow for a faithless soul.

Journey

So here it is, this is where life's taken me,

The secret that smiles , it's my awareness

That's hurting my existence, my friend, my nemesis!

My mind marches on, crushing my mere protestations,

The walls that close in are my solace

Yet, they enslave me, conscience where do you hide?

I have forgiven and so I'm forsaken,

How do my sins grow, do they play in vain?

The lust, the fear, the shame, the blame,

Like rain they flow, like fire they scorch

Eternal hopes shine , brighter than the flame!

Ode to you ....imperfect rock

Ode to you ….imperfect rock

For your endless patience, your burden of gravity

For your meagre signs of exasperations

For your subtle touches of forgiveness

For your gift of life and tears of death.

Ode to you….imperfect souls

For your eternal struggles, your innocent smiles

For your everlasting hope, your ethereal ideals

For your selfish dreams and hopeful revolutions

For your act of divinity, your suffocating rules & your.

Silent sighs.

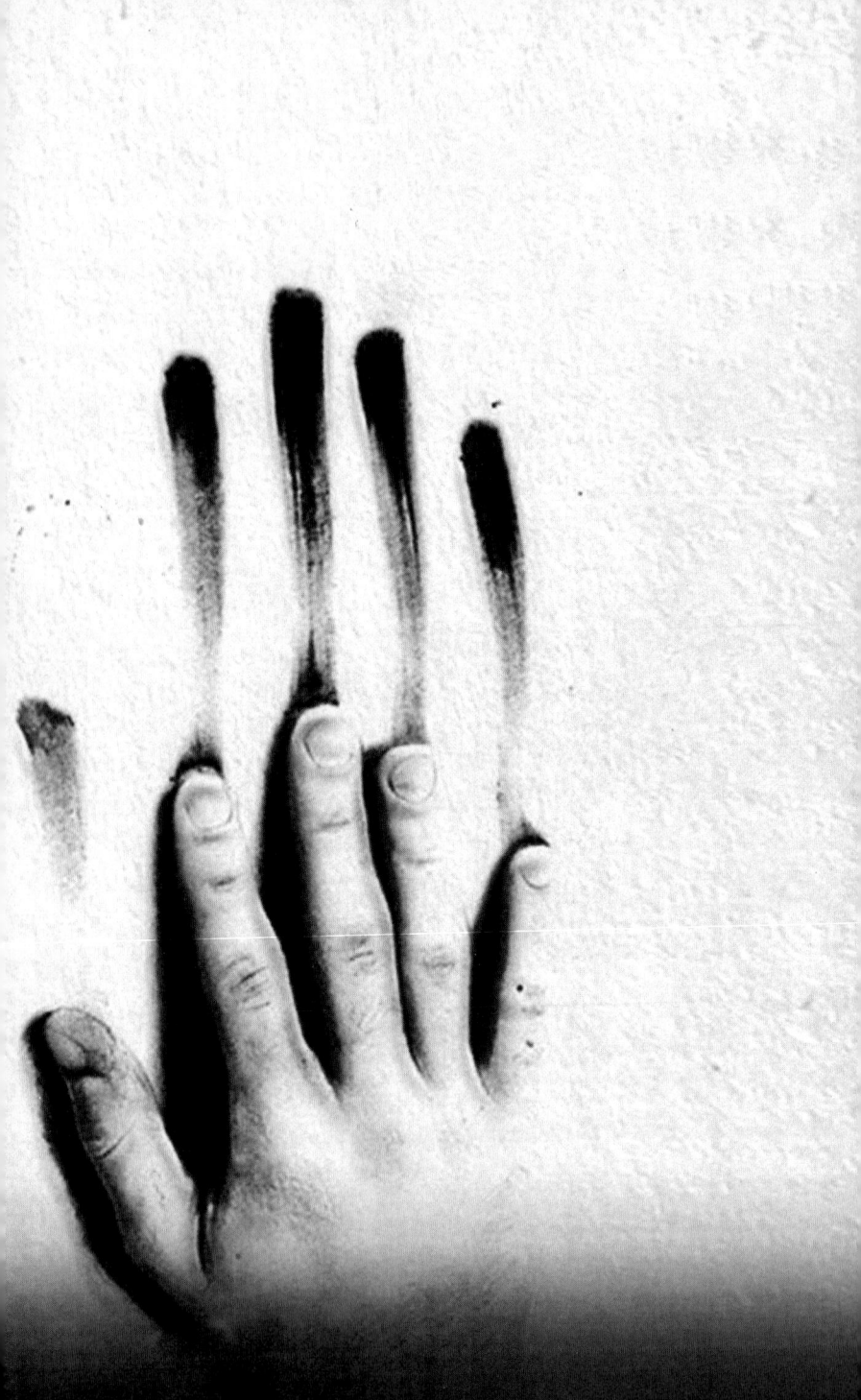

Eternal Wars

These wars that you fight, these wars within you,

These endless struggles that you endure through your patient lies,

And your fake smiles, while your conscience burns….

These tears that that lie enslaved in your deepest dungeons

Your pride lies hidden within your clenched fists

And songs of freedom play in infinite loops as the last light fades….

In dawn you smell the mist, the marks of tears paint your face

You feel reckless ambitions shatter your listless fears

Your steel breaks through these stubborn walls Against the storm, you stand tall

Against the filth and fire, faith shines through

For the wanderers, vagabonds & dreamers, their hopes eternal!

Fantasies in Utopia

If forgiveness was free and sins were wild imaginations,

I'd knock your unbreakable door till my patience bled

I'd cover myself with the cloak of unending expectations

And wait endlessly till the first light of day shone on my eyes.

If faith lay hidden in the words written on fragile prayers

I'd be the king of the world and walk away from my throne

I'd open every cage and fly into the utopian wilderness

And meditate with my eyes wide open without fear of judgement.

If freedom could heal your wounds lost in your lying smile

I'd break every chain till your reckless dreams lit up my unlit skies

I'd break every rule, unwrite every law, question every reason

And tear down every wall that you built to hide your broken soul.

If the world was free from your reckless inconsistencies

I'd hold your hand when they curse your thoughts

I'd save your stories from the pages that they burn

And sing out loud your tender notes that lie trampled tonight!

Broken Masks

Your sermons are lies

Your words reek of impossibility

While I hide behind this veil of invincibility

These wrinkles tell me the stories of my desperations

And memories pull me back

To the days of bliss….

Don't preach about life's unfairness

Of natural justice and faith

For I have seen through my faithless eyes

The naked hopes of men blinded by religion

While the children die….

Don't take my tears away

For they cleanse my empty soul

Through their prisms I see colours

Before darkness falls on these sleepless eyes…..

Don't heal my suffering

For they fuel my existence

And reignite my humanity

They tell me I'm still alive

While the walls close in……

Surrender

I seek peace

Where once there was love.

As justice smiles, A success at last.

Your triumphant gaze Bears me down.

Your fire burns In a brilliant rage.

Convicted, I stand before you,

Insignificant penitence!

No healing for my doubts,

No excuse for my curses.

Yet it's you,

I seek through these eternal waves.

The Vanquished

Your perfect hatred, glows like a beacon
My endless destruction, in search of a shore,
Your abundant glory, your victory, your song
My broken hopes, my desperations.
Your triumphant march, destiny in your hands
My shattered tears, scattered they lie,
Your gaze of a conqueror, fortune's your slave
My chained illusions, my clueless existence.

Idle Offerings

Oh Faith for my faithless soul,

I search for your dishonest embrace.

These years of torment, blinded by isolation,

A vision, clouded by the mist of listless dreams.

For the desperations of mere survival,

Where existence crumbles every moment.

Your ornate philosophies smell like worthless junk,

As the struggles evaporate before their ridiculed smirks.

I seek no forgiveness, my penance seeks no seal,

When our world's merge, for you I'll offer my imperfections.

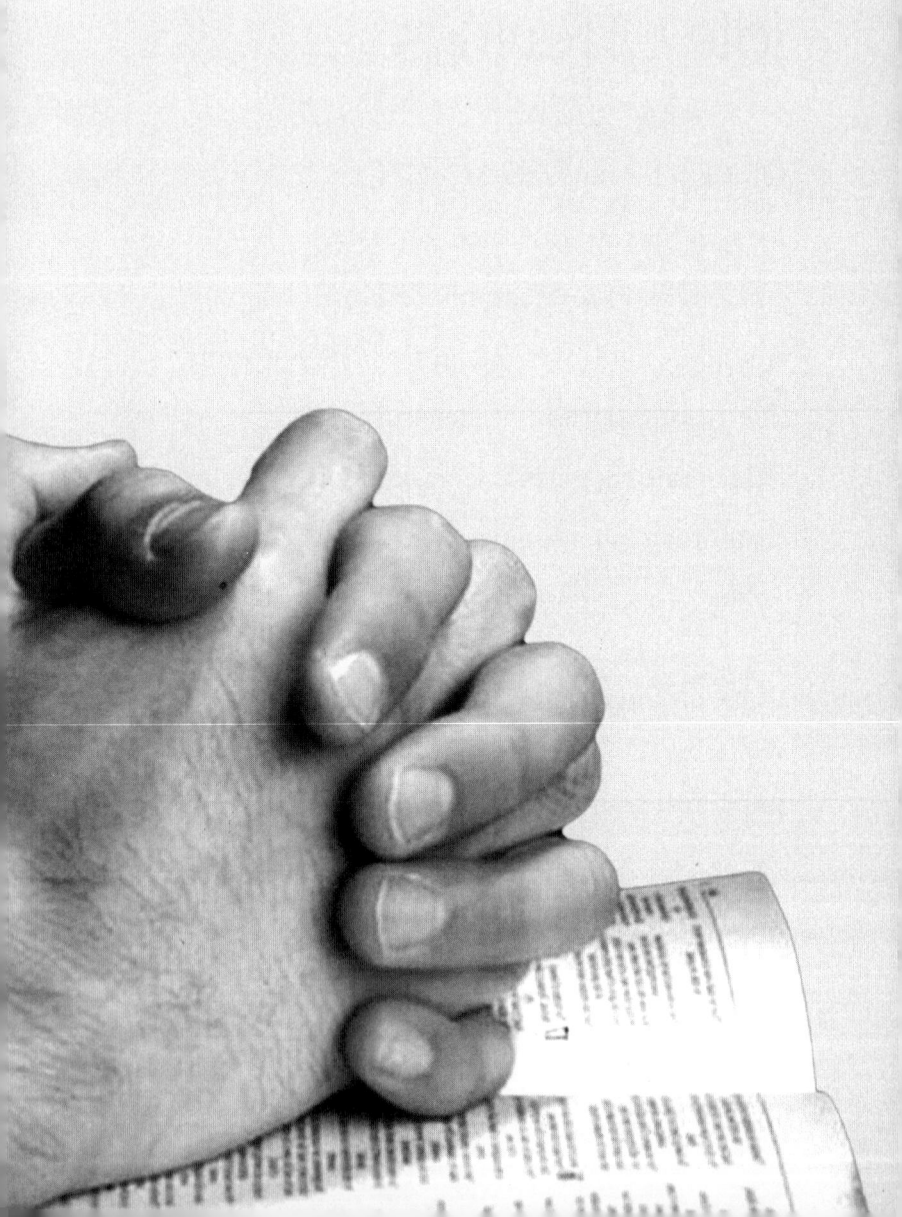

Confessions of the Faithless

My confessions, my acts of cowardice

When corrupt logic ruled my soul

I stand before you, Guilty, no more!

In these times of broken hope and endless prayer,

You stand accused and so I, Judge you

As a free man would, a fellow sinner!

Your rituals, your sycophancy, your dishonest smiles

Your strategies and politics, they lie flat.

Is this human, incomplete are we?

Our derailed expectations empty our minds,

Our greed smiles without shame,

Our gutless faith, will we rise or wither away?

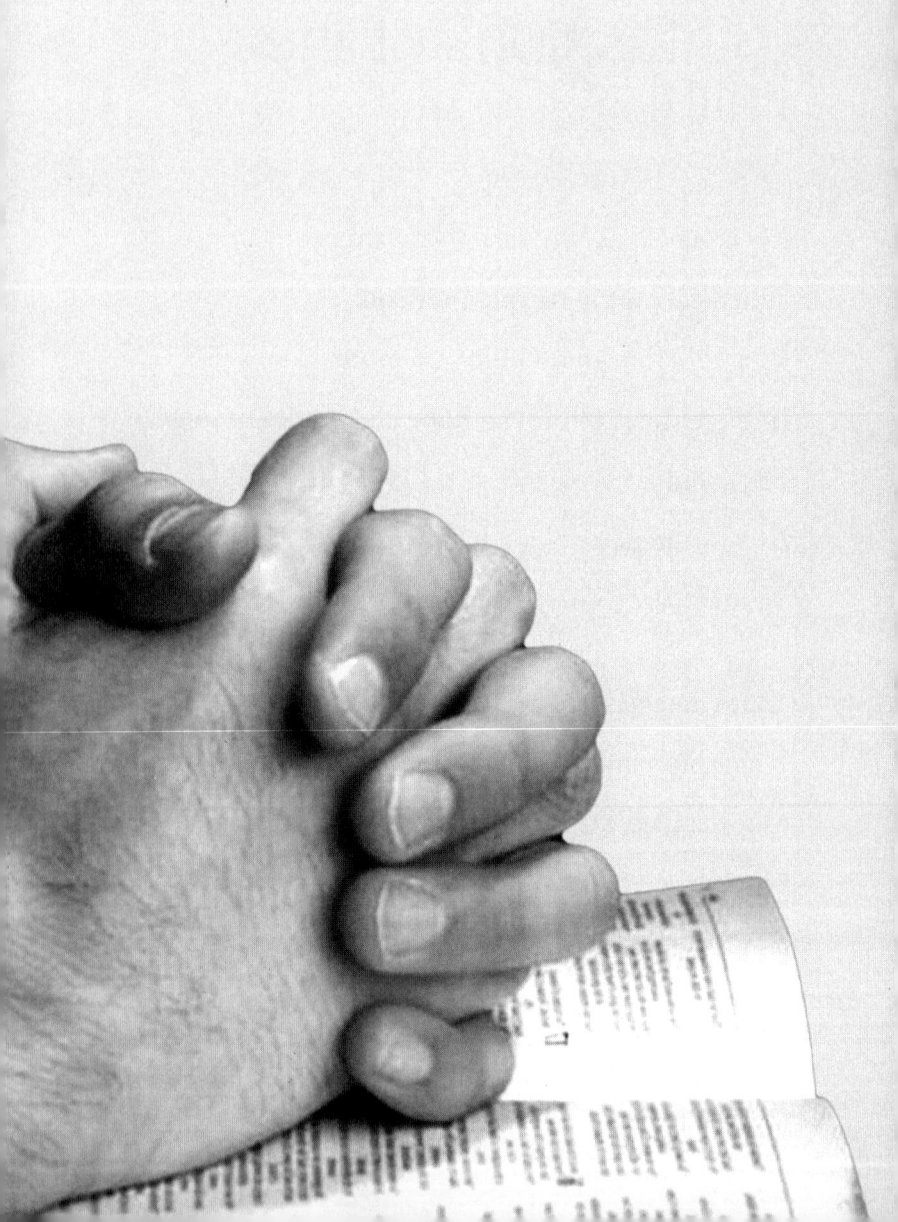

Confessions 1

I wear a cloak of tyranny in my kingdom of hell,

I've trampled on broken dreams and laughed at your pain.

In darkness, I've built my kingdom of blind zeal

I've shaped a grand world of eternal wounds.

Justice lies extinct, conscience drowned in a sea of hatred

Faith, covered in mortal dust, the path too lost to tread.

Your calls of mercy forever ignored in my invincible castle of glass

My arrogance stands strong, happiness traded for misery.

Do you see the tears that I have shed, for your breathless curses

In my heaven of sins, I lie alone, my strength abandoned!

My eyes scan the night sky for a speck of peace

In my dreams I lie in the arms of forgiveness.

Neglected Hopes

When these blank pages call out in desperation
And inspiration is lost in these dreary eyes
Questions crawl on the steps of existence
Neglected breaths discover lost tunes.
The tender touch of time taunts reality
As lost ambitions look for a place to hide
A bouquet of failed desires haunt memories
Fearless confessions knock the fragile door.
Truth and lies embraced in eternal conflict
Boundless joy smiles, intoxicated by listless love
The soul lies still as the embers glow
A restless heart yearns for a new dawn.

The wait

For endless nights I've waited to hear your footsteps
When our broken home will awake in our embrace
These tears will not hide in their dungeons
A distant smile will touch these parched lips.

The feeble cries of lost years will fade
The mind will erase the burden of pain
The dust of frozen curses will fly
My trembling hands will break these walls of darkness.

These unwritten letters in bliss will greet
Your memories still alive in every fragile word
Incomplete poems will search for your inspiration
In the canvas of dreams my imagination will take flight.

I watch with my sleepless eyes
As the fireflies cheer me in desperation
The stars, they call me to their cradle
In your return, my patience will find its destiny.

Farewell Song

Farewell my friend, the hour's close, the mist grows weak

I hear freedom's bugle call as my journey ends.

I come to hold your hand and sing lost songs

My debts repaid, my lost dreams forgotten.

Tomorrow, the unknown paths will welcome me

No strings will hold me back, no bond will enslave.

Let my heart be filled with the gift of broken memories

I'll hold them dear in the sea of emptiness.

The World will forget in its careless whims

And these worn-out lines will turn to dust.

When your eyes search for the days bygone

Remember the times of our innocent laughter.

Farewell my friend, my war has come to an end

Perhaps in these unknown lanes, our paths will cross again…

Untitled

My broken mind lies on the carpet of surrender

My rusted war-chest emptied by shrivelled hands

Faded hopes shine, masked by the fake smiles

Irrational dreams forgotten in fathomless rapture.

Thirst quenched by your sceptre of ridicule Mercy,

I've spread , over your unforgiving minds

My songs sung without the fear of judgement

Caressed by the breeze, I fall into the arms of the Sun.

The skeleton of ambitions rest on my shadows

My eyes wide awake as illusions fall apart

My conscious soul shines in innocent splendour

Through these times of turmoil, I'll find my path of solitude.

The Broken

Through my spotless arguments, I've built perfection

My legendary exploits lie carved in lifeless stones

I've built and ruled my world with dreams of deceit

My spotless freedom lost in fading ink stains.

I've read a million pages, spread words of illusion

Crafted unfathomable thoughts in my indestructible castle

In religion I see a weapon, in my reflections I see immortality

As I sway in the fragrance of endless power, my eyes grow blind.

The joy of life long forgotten, my mask of lies shine bright

I've run from the wails of faceless souls, from human touch

My inescapable justice glows and tramples upon weary dissent

My excuses search for air, my curses grow strong.

In the days of dark shadows, your broken home glows

Untouched by hunger, unmoved by injustice

You run from the spotlight, you soar in unsullied joy

The bliss of heaven in your eyes, vanquished by your forgiveness.

Days & Nights

As morning wakes into the lights of hope
The spirit of invincibility bathes my mind
Fearless ambitions float in endless glory
The World waits for my triumphant gaze.
Into the scorching noon the day drags
As doubts creep into my restless soul
Tired desires surrender to weary eyes
The hours remain, the way's unlost, yet!
With the setting Sun, restless faith flees
Ceaseless desires suffocate in the web of reality
Courage gives way to feeble desperations
As broken promises smile in hibernation.
The sound of tears lost as the crickets sing
As I lay stunned by the injustice of silence
In the stars I search for indifferent excuses
Dawn's near, so I dive into the ocean of dreams…..

Faceless Union

Your smile flows into my shameless tears
Broken time questions baffled conscience.
Decaying emotions fight for survival
As the bewildered lover plays with reason.
My burnt soul healed by your tender touch
My worries float in the waves of the universe.
Words fill the pages with whispers of silence
Infinite tranquility bathes in the fleeting moment.
Your touch of forgiveness frees my shackles
My bonds broken by hands of destiny.
My trembling hands reach out as faith calls
As colours splash the canvas of my restless heart.
Forgotten songs fly with reckless spirit
Endless peace soars in the chorus of birds.
My chamber of secrets unlocked
My pages swayed by the rhythm of your name.

Unburdened

My frozen desires take flight

Into dust fades my secret arrogance

Broken memories washed away in the rain
Misguided expectations turn to emptiness.

Time takes a backward step

No fear stalks the book of rules

No transactions for the worried soul

No burden of revolutions to bear.

My distant home , forgotten, My bonds of illusion, lost

Into the songs of the lost horizon, my evanescent footprints tread

Yet I see a speck of desire shine out in desperation

Still fenced by a glimpse of your helpless smile.

Meandering...

These next few lines…

These bleed for me,

For my selfish needs

They will follow no rules

They will flow like a listless river

They cry out loud, the sounds unheard.

The fears of tomorrow engulf me

Smothering me in my sleep

My prayers lie scattered

Forgiveness raises its valiant head

Tender memories play like wounds

Imprisoned in my hollow prison, time beckons mercy.

Innocent hopes prick my senses

Failed ambitions die endlessly

Sermons hide behind curses

My work still unfinished

Your blessings afraid to touch me

Silence embraces me, oblivious of its existence.

The lost road

These lost paths painted by your hands

My bewildered mind searched for direction

Fragmented dreams call out your name.

The home shivers like a shadow, abandoned

Judgements bow before silence

These tears cry locked in deep crevices.

These wounds lie free of guilt

Washed by waves of forgiveness

Faithless calls die in persistent neglect.

The distant horizon, still bathed in fantasy

Plays tricks on my tired legs

The Sun ,in all its shyness, peeks.

My eyes search for lost travellers

My stories yearn for an audience

And stars wake up to the momentary song.

As the tide of time washes my footprints

And my ceaseless journey soars

Your presence lies in wait.

Stan!

A few more years and I'll be hundred..

Though my hands shake and my eyes grow weak

Stay, and I'll show you my dreams

Your faith still flows strong in my veins.

Through the blessings of these prison walls

My mind drifts, my faith floats

My broken body hides its secrets

As I lay under freedom's torn blanket.

Though justice crawls on the roads of cowardice

Your smiles keep these shackles invisible

Through the hazy mist humanity often vanishes

While memories play games with my dried tears.

A few more years ,when I'll be hundred..

When we meet under the free skies

Will your fickle hearts remember

When I'll walk amongst you again?

Stan Swamy – Social reformer and activist (India). Died of old age and apathy of the "Authorities". He was jailed for several months. "In October 2020, Swamy filed for bail on the grounds of him being a victim of Parkinson's disease. His bail pleas were rejected multiple times. On 6 November 2020, Swamy submitted an application to the special court requesting a straw and sipper, stating that he was unable to hold a glass due to Parkinson's. In response to the delay in arranging a straw and a sipper for Swamy, social media users protested by ordering straws and sippers online, get- ting them delivered to the NIA's Mumbai office and at the Taloja jail – Wikipe- dia". He was 84…

Finding Hope..

I'm trying, I'm falling, I'm failing Hope's playing its eternal tricks

My sand castle and I, inseparable!

Tomorrow, I'll be reckless

Tonight, hope will caress

Guilts gentle blanket, still warm.

Lessons learnt will be forgotten

Sighs will face ruthless reality

Yesterday's Sins will be forgiven.

Strange lines will fill these pages

Unable to find directions

Ending in perfect desperations.

Vague ambitions will falter

Unsure of hidden perfections

Crumbled pages of history swallow hope.

In Search of Reasons

I rest on these fragile fields

And hear the mournful songs of time

The broken soul searches for peace

Consoled by the garden of dreams.

My aimless laments float

They hide in the narrow lanes

As rains cry out for directions

I run in search of memories adrift.

Weary sorrows demand justice

Justice plays with worn out excuses

The ragged mind sings songs of passion

As the tears turn blind.

The World sleeps under the cover of mercy

Embraced by the haze of guilt

Engulfed by empty affections

My vagabond eyes grow restless.

Conversation with Walls

These patient walls are my audience

Silently they listen, my stories of joy & desperations

My wails of endless protestations

Their sighs in perfect harmony.

The unruly wind surrenders

As it begs to break every rule

I ignore the ceaseless calls of the crickets

And search for songs lost in these fragile pages.

The poems recite their secret farewell

Their burden too heavy for another day

They beg for their last forgiveness

Only to be tangled in selfish pangs of solitude.

I search for existence as the lights dim

Unfaithful smiles play their usual tricks

These empty eyes wait for the dawn

The night hides in its usual neglect.

Lashings of Guilt

My existence in denial

In these moments of bliss

Interrupted by a lost tune

Waking my lost conscience.

A gust of guilt played havoc

Drawn by the faces of hungry children

And in the tears of helpless mothers

I see broken dreams float in soft neglect.

The shameless stage mocks sanity

The applause draped in careful deceit

As the doors close to blind promises

Reality gets taunted by the whips of illusion.

Hazy shades of triumph lie abandoned

Your faithless ovations fade in incoherence

My mind cries out for a touch of mercy

A speck of compassion on this weary road…

Kabul

The distant thunder rumbles

As freedom takes its final bow

Shackles and whips wake from their slumber

Justice is a coward tonight.

Mothers weep as sons fall

Prayers wrapped in anguish

Do you see death in your children's eyes

Do you seek forgiveness in their tears?

Hope is a listless wanderer

A traitor that long fled

No friend will hold my hand

No religion for my faith will shine.

Welcome , my conqueror

Dwell in your fleeting invincibility

My lying eyes embrace your justice

The mind caresses freedom's last breath.

The 2021 fall of Kabul, which came to be known as the fall of the Islamic Republic of Afghanistan, was the capture of Afghanistan's capital city of Kabul by the Taliban on 15 August 2021, the culmination of a military offensive which began in May 2021. The city's capture prompted an international airlift of fleeing civilians and took place hours after President Ashraf Ghani fled the country.

Lost Conscience

Have you heard the mother's cry in her broken home

And deftly ignored the calls of your soul

Do the lies cover your face of remorse

In the eyes of the children, have you felt the pangs of hunger?

Are you still swayed by the brilliant illusions

Do your hands embrace the cold touch of injustice

Do your blindfolds shatter a million dreams

And sleep in peace while your conscience burns?

In your mirrors do you see new faces

Do the burden of sin wear you down

Your sermons, do they still sound hollow

Are you touched by the unfelt touch of forgiveness/ Mercy?

Have you travelled to your innocent cradle

In the stars have you lost your existence

Do the songs of solitude still touch your lips

Have you searched for the hues of the hidden moon?

If you find yourself wandering on the roads unknown

Through these broken rays of time I shall return…

Lost Reminiscence

It is that time of the year

When hope strays into the unknown

And your ruthless absence in cold embrace

Its voice drenched in feeble protestations.

Morning has strayed into emptiness

Its colours fade as it grows

And the broken mirror cries in vain

At the sight of fragmented images.

The evening breeze has lost its way

No tired songs of birds greet the dusk

Silent lies the spotless sky

Hollow doors greet the tired feet.

The stars in careless silence

They hear the words of surrender

Darkness engulfs, its reins torn

These eyes play traitor as thoughts fade…

The Poet

He stares at the empty pages
of the thoughts that his mind explores
only to evaporate when he holds his rickety pen.
He has a dream, someday the world will
wonder why his words never made any sense
and unforgiving minds will forever curse.
He often wakes up at the sound of tears
surrounded by wondrous ambitions
which gaze at him momentarily.
He gathers hope from faint desperations
and unlearnt lessons that don't blink
when ruthless eyes judge without remorse.

Price of Existence

The price of existence

Unquestioned aimlessness

In awe of faceless ambitions

Let me float in ignorance.

Drowning in unknown complexities

My thoughts in silent revolt

My scars carefully masked

My mind absorbed in absurdity.

Words of wisdom flutter

And fade from my imperfect grasp

To be cursed by forgiveness

Treasures forgotten in insanity.

Fragile possessions not afraid to fly

Gentle hopes bathed in flawed curiosity

Hold hands as they flicker in ecstasy

Emptiness beckons, it's rays in rare splendour.

Contradictions

My sins draped in honest virtues
I exist, yet I'm wilfully bare.
My splendour washed in unforgiving desolation
A million dreams drown in my blind eyes.
These curses caressed by the touch of grace
My absolute freedom still reeks of bondage.
My wrecked ambitions in harmony with hope
The vagabond soul searches for a home.
In untainted silence I hear cries of despair
And quench my thirst in the gentle mirage.
In my selfish garden generosity blooms
On my wings of peace I carry wrecking storms.
My fearless ways veiled by cowardice
I am the night touched by dawns divine glow.

The Lies within Us

My tangled mind in utter disarray
Your professed faith drowned by ruthless reasons
Bright festival lights glow another night
And into the morning they toil aimlessly.
Miracles draped in illusion are a minority
Freedom chokes in the smoke of deceit
Prayers drowned in the rough seas
Yet the stubborn cries of ragged hope persist.
In my unspoken desperations
I lay awake, engulfed by unwoven dreams
Words float as boats on endless rivers
The cries of the shore lost in the mist.
Silence, once a distant blessing
Threatens like a torturous fiend
Where hope is a casualty of luxury
I hear faint whispers of withering desires.

Ruins

Like lovers from two cursed worlds
We float in clouds of disarray
United by transient tenderness
Touched by waves of isolation.
Lost in undying desperations
Bathed in the cold rays of deception
Prayers locked in lost dungeons
Yet touched by stubborn hope.
Pride flees from the veils of death
The breath of life flows in silence
Whips fly in subdued anger
Wounds forgive brutal fangs
Existence blooms from blind innocence
Intoxicated by balms of apathy
Stronger we soar across boundaries
Where our solitary roads will unite.

Acknowledgements

Sincere thanks to my Literary Agent – "The Book Bakers" and especially to Suhail Mathur for giving me this opportunity to explore my creative side and for the immense help that I have received in this exhilarating publishing journey. I would also like to thank my Publisher, Anecdote Publishing House for their incredible support and guidance.